BLACK and WHITE
Animals

Skunks

by Mari Schuh

CAPSTONE PRESS
a capstone imprint

Little Pebble is published by Capstone Press,
1710 Roe Crest Drive, North Mankato, Minnesota 56003
www.mycapstone.com

Library of Congress Cataloging-in-Publication Data
Library of Congress Cataloging-in-Publication Data is available on the Library of Congress website.

ISBN 978-1-5157-3622-6 (hardcover)
ISBN 978-1-5157-3624-0 (paperback)
ISBN 978-1-5157-3626-4 (eBook PDF)

Summary: Learn about skunks!

Editorial Credits
Gena Chester, editor; Kayla Rossow, designer; Morgan Walters, media researcher;
Kathy McColley, production specialist

Photo Credits
Dreamstime: Rancho, 17; Getty Images: Daniel J Cox, 11, John Cancalosi, 21, Leonard Lee Rue III, 19; iStockphoto: Holly Kuchera, 9; Shutterstock: Bildagentur Zoonar GmbH, 7, critterbiz, cover, Curly Pat, design element cover, Debbie Steinhausser, 13, Heiko Kiera, 5, James Coleman, 1, Markovka, design element throughout, Yasmins world, backcover; SuperStock: Minden Pictures, 15

Table of Contents

A Bad Smell

A bad smell fills the air.

Look!

It's a skunk!

Skunks are black and white.

The colors warn animals.

Back off!

Skunks hiss when
danger is near.
They stamp their feet.

Skunks raise their bushy tails.

They spray musk.

Look out!

Musk is stinky.
The smell keeps
predators away.

Night and Day

Skunks live alone.

At night they hunt.

They eat mice and fish.

They eat eggs too.

Skunks dig.

They find bugs to eat.

Yum!

Skunks sleep in dens
during the day.
They line dens with leaves.
Their homes are warm.

Glossary

bushy—thick and fluffy

den—a place where a wild animal may live; a den can be underground, in hollow logs, or under buildings

hiss—to make a "sss" sound like a snake

hunt—to chase and kill animals for food

musk—an oil that skunks spray when they sense danger

predator—an animal that hunts other animals for food

stomp—to bang your foot down

Read More

Bowman, Chris. *Striped Skunks*. North American Animals. Minneapolis: Bellwether Media, 2016.

Gray, Susan H. *Skunks Smell Bad.* Tell Me Why. Ann Arbor, Mich.: Cherry Lake Publishing, 2015.

Shoemaker, Kate. *Skunk Stench*. Nature's Grossest. New York: Gareth Stevens Publishing, 2015.

Internet Sites

FactHound offers a safe, fun way to find internet sites related to this book. All of the sites on FactHound have been researched by our staff.

Here's all you do:
Visit *www.facthound.com*
Type in this code: 9781515736226

Super-cool stuff! Check out projects, games and lots more at
www.capstonekids.com

Critical Thinking Using the Common Core

1. What is a den? (Craft and Structure)

2. Why do you think skunks hunt at night? How might hunting at night be easier than hunting during the day? (Integration of Knowledge and Ideas)

3. Name some ways skunks scare away predators. (Key Ideas and Details)

Index